From PhD to Purpose: The Unexpected Path

From PhD to Purpose: The Unexpected Path

A Journey of Hope, Community, and Choosing to Go All In

HEZRON OTTEY

RESOURCE *Publications* • Eugene, Oregon

FROM PHD TO PURPOSE: THE UNEXPECTED PATH
A Journey of Hope, Community, and Choosing to Go All In

Resource Publications
An Imprint of Wipf and Stock Publishers
199 W. 8th Ave., Suite 3
Eugene, OR 97401

www.wipfandstock.com

PAPERBACK ISBN: 979-8-3852-5334-0
HARDCOVER ISBN: 979-8-3852-5335-7
EBOOK ISBN: 979-8-3852-5336-4
VERSION NUMBER 08/21/25

To my wife, Paula, and our daughter, Keanna—
Your unwavering support and belief in me have been a source of enormous strength. This book is as much yours as it is mine.

To Professor Peter Kevern—
Your guidance and mentorship throughout my PhD journey shaped both my work and the way I see the world. I am deeply grateful for your wisdom and encouragement.

Contents

Preface

THIS BOOK IS THE RESULT of a journey I never expected to take, one marked by uncertainty, rejection, and ultimately, faith. When I set out on my path through academic research, community work, and personal reflection, I had a vision of success shaped by conventional standards. But life has a way of reshaping our perspectives.

At times, I questioned my purpose, wondering if my efforts were leading anywhere meaningful. Yet, in the quiet moments, I began to see that God was guiding me all along, not through dramatic signs but through the steady unfolding of events, the people he placed in my path, and the work that had been growing right in front of me.

The lessons within these pages are not just theoretical. They are lived experiences shaped by the realities of rejection, perseverance, and discovering fulfilment in unexpected places. Through my work with Telford Community Basketball and my academic journey, I have come to see that success is not defined by titles or recognition but by alignment with God's purpose.

I wrote this book for anyone who has ever felt lost, discouraged, or uncertain about their path. If you have ever questioned whether your efforts matter or wondered if you are on the right track, I hope this book serves as both a reassurance and an encouragement. Faith is not just about reaching a destination; it is about trusting the one who leads the way.

Thank you for joining me on this journey.

Introduction

I THOUGHT THAT EARNING a PhD would be the final piece of the puzzle.

I imagined the moment—walking across the stage, shaking hands, the weight of my achievement settling in. I had spent years researching, writing, and pushing through sleepless nights to reach this point. Surely, this was it. The moment everything would fall into place.

I was wrong.

Instead of a flood of job offers, I faced a wall of silence. Application after application vanished into the void. Emails went unanswered. Interviews felt promising, but the rejections came anyway.

Weeks turned into months. The excitement of graduation faded into frustration. Doubt crept in. Had I wasted years of my life chasing something that wasn't meant for me?

I had done everything right. I had the qualifications, the experience, the determination. And yet, the world didn't seem to care.

I wasn't just unemployed. I felt invisible.

But while my career dreams stalled, something else was quietly growing.

Since 2019, I had been running a small, non-competitive basketball initiative in my community—just a simple space where people could come together, stay active, and feel a sense of belonging. It wasn't about competition or trophies. It was about connection.

At first, it was just that—a passion project, a way to give back, to create something positive. But as my job search dragged on, I started to see it differently.

While chasing a career, I had already built something real, something meaningful.

Every week, I saw people—of all backgrounds, faiths, and ages—finding joy, friendship, and confidence on that court. I saw people who had never been part of a team before stepping up as leaders. I saw people struggling with loneliness finding a place where they belonged.

And then it hit me.

I had been waiting for someone to give me an opportunity when, all along, I had already created one.

So, I made a decision.

On March 17, 2025, I officially registered Telford Community Basketball as a Community Interest Company (CIC). No longer just a side project, this was something bigger; something built to last.

This book is about that journey. The rejections. The uncertainties. The fear of feeling as if I had nothing, only to realize I had everything that I needed right in front of me.

It's about finding purpose in the unexpected. About faith, resilience, and trusting that, even when things don't go according to plan, the right path is still unfolding.

Because when one door doesn't open, maybe you were never meant to walk through it in the first place. Maybe you were meant to build your own.

LEVEL A

The Climb

Earning a PhD

Theme: Hard Work, Sacrifice, and Expectations

Chapter 1

The Dream That Kept Me Going

THE DREAM STARTED LONG before I even fully understood what it meant. It wasn't born overnight, nor did it emerge from a single moment of clarity. It was a slow burn, a persistent voice that whispered in the background of my life, growing louder with each passing year. It was the dream of a future that I couldn't fully grasp but could feel with every fiber of my being—a future where my work would matter, where my research could change lives, where my passion would fuel progress. The journey to my PhD wasn't just about earning an academic title; it was about fulfilling a greater purpose, one I felt deep inside me.

There were many moments where that dream seemed more like a distant star twinkling in the night sky—beautiful and bright but far beyond my reach. But I couldn't shake the belief that it was meant for me, that I was meant for something more, something bigger. I wasn't content with simply existing, drifting from day to day. I wanted to leave a mark. I wanted to make a difference. And the PhD was the path that would lead me there.

I remember the first time that I seriously considered pursuing a doctorate. It wasn't something I had always known that I wanted, but when the idea took root, it felt like a lightning bolt, like a surge of energy that coursed through me. I wasn't sure exactly what the path would look like, but I knew I couldn't back down. I had to take the plunge. I had a vision—a powerful, burning belief that by the time I reached the end of my PhD, I would have the knowledge and skills to do something transformative. And that belief became my fuel.

But pursuing a PhD is no easy task. No one talks about the quiet struggles, the sacrifices that come with this kind of ambition. No one prepares you for the isolation that follows you through late nights and early mornings, when the world is asleep but you're wide awake, lost in the sea of research and deadlines. It's a journey that requires more than just intellect—it demands everything that you have. It's the kind of commitment that means waking up before dawn to write, to research, to think. It's the kind of persistence that means spending hours dissecting theories, reviewing articles, writing and rewriting, and pushing through the constant mental fatigue that comes with the process.

There were moments when I wanted to quit. There were days when the weight of the work felt suffocating, when my mind screamed for a break, but my body refused to allow it. There were nights when I would sit at my desk, staring at a blinking cursor, unable to produce anything meaningful. I questioned myself—my abilities, my choices. I asked, *Is this really worth it?* But then, in the quietest moments, something would click. A thought would align, a concept would make sense, and the fog would clear for a moment. And, in that brief moment of clarity, I would remember why I started. It wasn't just for the degree; it was for the greater purpose, for the impact I wanted to make. That belief was a lifeline, pulling me forward, giving me strength when I thought that I had none left.

The long nights were filled with tears, frustration, and self-doubt. But they were also filled with moments of brilliance, of discovery, of seeing my research come to life in ways that I hadn't anticipated. Those breakthroughs—however small they seemed—were like the first rays of sunlight after a long, dark storm. And with each small victory, my belief grew stronger. I was closer to my goal. Closer to the dream that had kept me going.

And as I moved closer to the finish line, that belief crystallized: *once I graduate, everything will fall into place.* That was my mantra. I clung to it. The thought that all the sacrifice would be worth it, that somehow all the pieces would come together, and the world would recognize my hard work. The grind would end, and I would finally have the freedom to create the future that I envisioned. It was a powerful thought, a comforting thought. And it kept me going.

REFLECT AND REIMAGINE

1. What story have you been telling yourself about success?

   Take a moment to reflect on the narrative you've been living by. Is your definition of success rooted in someone else's expectations? If you stripped away titles, accolades, and external validation, what would success mean to *you*?

2. What seeds have you already planted that could grow into something extraordinary?

   Sometimes we overlook the quiet work we've been doing because it doesn't fit society's picture of achievement. Pause and ask yourself: *What have I already created whether in my relationships, passions, or contributions that holds meaning and potential?*

3. Are you waiting for permission to step into your purpose?

   Think about the moments when you've held back, waiting for validation or approval from others before moving forward. What would happen if you stopped waiting today? How would your life change if you trusted that you're already equipped to create something meaningful?

4. How can rejection become a turning point in your story?

   Rejection often feels final, but what if it's actually pointing you toward something better? Reflect on a time when rejection left you questioning your worth—could it have been redirecting you toward something uniquely suited to your purpose? How might embracing rejection as redirection reshape how you approach challenges?

5. What impact are you making right now that aligns with your values?

   Success isn't always loud or obvious. It's often found in the quiet ways we touch lives and build connections. Look at your current journey: How are your choices reflecting your values? What legacy are you already building through the lives you touch and the communities you nurture?

Chapter 2

Graduation: The High Before the Drop

THE DAY HAD ARRIVED. The day that had been years in the making. Graduation—that moment when all the long hours, the sacrifices, the struggles, and the relentless pursuit of knowledge were supposed to pay off. It was the culmination of everything that I had worked for, everything that I had dreamed of. As I sat there, dressed in my cap and gown, waiting for my name to be called, it felt surreal. This was the moment that would define everything. The degree, the recognition—it was all right in front of me. I could almost taste it.

The ceremony was everything that I had imagined. The air was thick with excitement, a sense of pride and accomplishment hanging in the atmosphere. I remember the faces of my friends, family, and professors. They were all there to witness my achievement, and, in their eyes, I saw pride. I saw the reflection of the hard work that I had put in—and it felt good. I felt good. The applause as I walked across the stage was almost overwhelming. Each step I took was a victory, not just for me but for everyone who had supported me along the way. I had made it.

But then, as the ceremony ended, as the celebrations wound down, a strange emptiness began to seep in. There was this lingering feeling that didn't match the high I had expected to feel. The joy of finishing my PhD was palpable, but there was also a quiet, creeping doubt that slowly started to take root. The world had celebrated me. But was the world ready for me? Was I truly ready to face what came next?

The expectations were high, perhaps even unspoken. The sense of accomplishment felt so complete in that moment, but the reality quickly set in: What now? Graduation had been the climax, but I hadn't fully prepared for the drop that followed. I had worked for years, I had earned my place, but no one had warned me that the hardest part was yet to come. The world outside the academic bubble was a whole new beast—unpredictable, often indifferent, and far less structured than I had imagined.

I thought back to everything that had led me here—the years spent buried in research, chasing a question most people had never even considered.

My PhD was in Health and Welfare Studies—but more specifically—it explored the impact of Seventh-day Adventist beliefs, values, and practices on physical activity in the United Kingdom. It wasn't exactly a topic that made for casual dinner conversation.

Try explaining to someone that you've spent an entire week analyzing survey responses about levels of religious behavior and physical activity, only for a single anomaly in the data to throw everything into question. Or that you've combed through decades of denominational health literature, cross-referencing it with epidemiological studies, and trying to find a pattern, a connection, something undeniable.

At one point, I had spent thirty-five straight hours staring at data sets. Thirty-five hours. No real sleep—just a blur of numbers, patterns, and qualitative responses swimming in front of my eyes. I remember the dull hum of my laptop, the glow of the screen burning into my retinas, and the steady drip of green tea fuelling my resolve.

And what was I doing for all those hours? Coding—not in the way a software engineer does, but in the painstaking process of qualitative thematic analysis. Every sentence—every phrase—had to be categorized, cross-checked, and scrutinized for deeper meaning.

"I walk more on Sabbath because the members walk after potluck."

Code: Sabbath Observance—Indirect Influence on Physical Activity

"My faith encourages me to care for my body, but exercise feels less important than diet."

Code: Faith-Based Health Prioritization—Diet vs. Physical Activity

"I don't join the gym because of modesty concerns."

Code: Religious Values—Barriers to Public Exercise Spaces

Multiply that process by hundreds of responses across dozens of participants, and you start to get a picture of the kind of obsessive madness a PhD requires.

At one point, I remember jolting awake at my desk, my face pressed against a pile of articles about Blue Zones: regions of the world where people live longest, including Loma Linda, a Seventh-day Adventist community in California. I had fallen asleep mid-sentence, pen still in hand.

And this wasn't an isolated incident. This was my life for years—days and nights blurred together in an endless cycle of writing, analyzing, questioning, rewriting—all in pursuit of a conclusion that felt just beyond my grasp.

People assume a PhD is just an advanced degree, but they don't realize it's an obsession. It takes over your mind, your time, your sense of reality; it makes you forget to eat, forget you need sleep, forget there's a world outside your head.

So when I talked about my PhD when I held onto it as proof of worth, as something meant to guarantee my future, I wasn't just talking about an academic title. I meant years poured into sacrifice, exhaustion, belief, all hoping it'd mean something someday.

But what happens when it doesn't?

What happens when the world looks at all those hours, sleepless nights, and carefully-coded responses and says, "Not enough, not this time"?

That silence afterward overwhelmed me.

I thought graduation would be different; that it would fix all those doubts; that walking across that stage would erase every sleepless night or unanswered question about what came next.

But instead, as soon as reality set back in, I realized how little any degree could prepare me for what lay ahead.

I thought I was ready. The job market beckoned, and with my PhD in-hand I believed myself equipped-for-anything. Armed with confidence, I sent applications tailored perfectly, a polished CV, and personal cover letters. Then I hit "send," expecting floods of responses.

But days passed and responses weren't floods; they were droughts. Rejections piled higher than the dreams I'd imagined success bringing.

Hadn't all this work earned me anything?

Despite frustration, confusion, and doubt, I refused to let go of dreams chasing purpose.

REFLECT AND REFRAME

1. What expectations have you placed on yourself about success?

   Think about the moments when you've tied your worth to a title, degree, or achievement. Are those expectations truly yours, or have they been shaped by societal pressures? How might your life change if you allowed yourself to redefine success on your own terms?

2. What sacrifices have you made in pursuit of a goal, and were they worth it?

   Consider the long hours, sleepless nights, and personal costs you've endured to achieve something important. Did those sacrifices align with your values, or did they come at the expense of something deeper? How can you approach future goals with balance and intention?

3. How do you respond when the world doesn't meet your expectations?

Graduation often feels like a finish line, but what happens when reality doesn't match the dream? Reflect on how you've handled disappointment or setbacks in your life. Have they taught you resilience, redirected you toward something better, or left you questioning your path?

4. Where in your life are you already building something meaningful?

   Sometimes we're so focused on what's next that we miss what's already growing under our care. Look at your current projects, relationships, or passions—what seeds have you planted that could grow into something extraordinary if nurtured?

5. What would it look like to trust your journey even when it feels uncertain?

   Uncertainty is an inevitable part of transitions, but it can also be a space for growth and discovery. How might you embrace the unknown as an opportunity rather than a setback? What steps can you take today to move forward with courage and faith in what's ahead?

LEVEL B

The Fall

Job Search and the Crisis of Purpose

Theme: Rejection, Frustration, Redefining Self-Worth

Chapter 3

Silence Is the Loudest Sound

There's an eerie kind of silence that follows the submission of a job application. At first it feels innocent enough, just a moment of waiting. But after a few days, it begins to sink in. That silence? It isn't peaceful anymore. It's heavy. It feels like an echo reverberating, growing louder and louder, until it feels suffocating. Every time you check your email—and there's nothing—your chest tightens. Your breath quickens. You feel a small knot of anxiety forming in the pit of your stomach. And with each passing day, it gets harder to ignore.

I'd spent years working toward this moment: completing my PhD, delving into complex research, and sacrificing countless hours of my life in pursuit of something bigger. I had a vision of success, of stepping out into the world, ready to change it with my qualifications. Ready to make a difference. *I was ready*. The world should have been ready for me.

At least that's what I believed.

But then came the applications. At first, I sent them out with confidence. These were opportunities that I had prepared for, positions that were made for someone with my expertise. With optimism I hit "send," sure that it was only a matter of time before the calls came flooding in. After all, I had the qualifications. I had the passion. My academic journey wasn't just a degree; it was my story, my narrative of perseverance, dedication, and grit.

But the silence began to stretch.

The first few days after sending out each application felt normal. Maybe a little bit of hope and anticipation. But, after the first week, doubt started creeping in. Two weeks passed. Nothing. And then the crushing reality began to hit: I wasn't hearing back because I wasn't good enough. I wasn't even getting the courtesy of a "No, thank you." And that—the *absence* of response—was almost worse than rejection itself.

The silence became louder than any words. It haunted my every thought. In the stillness, my mind raced, spinning in circles. *Why wasn't I getting any feedback? What was wrong with me?* I could hear the question in my head like a mantra, asking me over and over again, gnawing at me. *Maybe I'm not as qualified as I thought? Maybe I don't have what it takes?* Those quiet, subtle whispers of self-doubt were overwhelming.

The longer the silence stretched on, the more I began to question my worth. I had always believed that hard work would eventually pay off, that the degree would open doors, and that all the sacrifices would amount to something tangible. I had followed all the rules. I had jumped through all the hoops. And yet, here I was—waiting for a sign that I wasn't invisible, that my efforts hadn't been in vain.

I remember sitting at my desk, staring at my inbox, my heart pounding, just waiting for that one email that would change everything. It never came. Each morning I would refresh my email like some kind of ritual, expecting to see the familiar ding of a response, hoping for the news that would finally prove that I had made it. But there was only emptiness. And the longer I waited, the more the silence began to speak to me, louder and louder. *You don't belong here. You're not good enough. Why did you ever think this would work?*

The quiet was crushing. And it didn't just stay confined to my inbox. The silence started creeping into my life. It followed me into conversations, into social situations. It settled on me like a thick fog. When people asked how my job search was going, I put on a smile, tried to sound upbeat, but inside the silence echoed. *They're waiting too. They're waiting for you to succeed. And you're failing them.*

The longer the silence stretched, the more I felt it shaping me, defining me. The world didn't care about my PhD. The world didn't see my qualifications. The world was telling me that I was irrelevant. I started to feel small, insignificant, as if I were a fleeting moment in a sea of endless noise. And there, in that silence, my sense of purpose began to erode. I had spent years chasing this elusive vision of success, only to find myself locked in this quiet, echoing space where nothing was happening. Where everything seemed out of reach.

And then, the moments that really stung were the nights when the doubt would keep me awake. I'd find myself scrolling through job boards late into the night, looking for something, anything. I kept seeing jobs that seemed perfect, jobs that were a direct match for my skills, for everything I had worked for. But when I clicked on the description, I was always met with the same message: "Applications closed." *Too late. Too slow. Never enough.*

The silence wasn't just about no responses; it was the *not knowing*. What was I doing wrong? Was I not qualified enough? Was my research too niche, too specialized? Or was it something deeper—was it that creeping fear that perhaps I wasn't cut out for the very thing that I had spent my life preparing for? Or was it that maybe this whole dream of having a meaningful career, of making an impact, was just a mirage?

Some nights I would lie in bed, staring at the ceiling, wondering if all of this was even worth it. I was getting older; the world was moving forward; and I felt stuck. Stuck in the same place, day after day, waiting for something that never seemed to come. The more I waited, the more I realized that my sense of identity had become wrapped up in this idea of success—the success that was supposed to come with a job, with validation, with the promise of a future that I had always dreamed of. But with every passing day, that future felt more distant, slipping further away.

The silence wasn't just in my inbox anymore. It was inside of me. It was in my bones. It became the loudest sound in my life, and it had nothing to do with what I could hear. It was, rather, all about what I couldn't.

And it's amazing how loud silence can be when it's the only thing you're left with.

REFLECT AND RECONNECT

1. How do you handle silence in your life?

   Think about the moments when you've faced uncertainty—whether in relationships, careers, or personal goals. How do you respond when answers don't come? Do you let silence define your worth, or can you find strength in the waiting?

2. What story are you telling yourself during moments of doubt?

   When silence stretches on, it's easy to let self-doubt take over. Are the thoughts running through your mind building you up? Or are they tearing you down? What would happen if you rewrote that internal narrative to reflect your resilience rather than your fears?

3. What does rejection mean to you?

   Rejection often feels like failure, but could it be redirection instead? Reflect on a time when rejection closed one door but opened another. How might embracing rejection as part of your journey change how you approach setbacks moving forward?

4. Where is your worth anchored?

   When external validation is absent—no responses, no feedback—where do you find your sense of value? Is it tied to accomplishments or titles, or does it come from something deeper within yourself? What steps can you take to anchor your worth in something unshakable?

5. What small actions can you take today to move forward?

   In moments of waiting, it's easy to feel stuck, but progress doesn't have to be grand or immediate. What small steps can you take right now to shift your focus from what's out of your control to what's within it? How might those steps help quiet the noise of doubt?

Chapter 4

Overqualified, Under-Experienced, Stuck

There's a strange paradox in the job market, one that I never expected to face. I thought that once I had my PhD, once I'd proven myself with years of research and academic rigor, the doors would open. I thought that the world would recognize the blood, sweat, and tears that I had poured into my work, and, in return, they'd give me a job, an opportunity. But what I didn't anticipate was this brutal, confusing dance with the job market, a dance where I was stuck in the middle, neither here nor there.

The first few weeks of the job search had been hopeful. With a sense of purpose, I sent out applications, fully believing that I had the edge. The qualifications, the passion, the hard-won knowledge—all of it made me feel as if I was more than ready to take on whatever role that I applied for. And yet, I quickly began to realize that I was now trapped in an inescapable cycle: *overqualified, under-experienced, and stuck.*

It started with the first few rejections—the polite, almost robotic emails which told me, in no uncertain terms, that I wasn't the right fit for the position. These rejections didn't sting at first; I was still fuelled by hope, by the belief that the right opportunity would come. It didn't. And when I looked deeper into the positions that I was applying for, I started to notice something that confused me even more—each one came with a different set of criteria, a different kind of expectation.

For some jobs, I was overqualified. I was applying for roles that would typically require someone with practical experience, or a few years in the field. And then I would see the job description where they were asking for someone with a master's degree and a couple of years of experience. My PhD screamed "too much." My qualifications were overwhelming, a double-edged sword that made me seem intimidating, out of reach.

I was the type of person who had spent years honing my craft, dissecting intricate theories, and diving deep into topics that few dared to touch. But, in the world of job applications, I had become a victim of my own expertise. They didn't need someone with my depth of knowledge. They needed someone who could hit the ground running, someone who had been there, done that, had the battle scars from the trenches.

I remember reading through a job description for a role that was *perfect* on paper—almost too perfect. The skills they were asking for were exactly what I had developed throughout my research. The job seemed tailor-made for someone like me, someone with a passion for community, for health, for making a tangible difference in the world. I could already picture myself in the role, collaborating with a team, strategizing, bringing my fresh ideas and experience to the table.

But then, buried in the middle of the description, was the deal-breaker: *must have at least two years of industry experience.* I had never worked in the industry. I had spent my time in academia refining my expertise, but that didn't count in their eyes. No matter how much I believed in the work I had done, no matter how much of an asset I knew that I could be, I was disqualified because of a lack of hands-on experience.

It was a punch to the gut.

And yet, at the same time, I was also hearing the opposite feedback from other roles—feedback that I wasn't experienced enough. I was told that, despite my impressive academic background, I lacked the practical skills that would make me effective in the role. In those moments, I felt as if I were being pulled in two different directions, and neither one was leading to a destination I wanted. I was neither qualified enough nor experienced enough. I was stuck in the middle, with no way out.

The internal battle was exhausting. I had built up this vision of what my life would look like after graduation—doors opening, the world welcoming me with open arms. Instead, I was confronted with this twisted paradox: I was too much for some positions, and not enough for others. No matter how hard I tried, no matter how much I bent and twisted, I couldn't make myself fit the mold that the job market was demanding.

The frustration intensified with every application, every rejection, every interview that went nowhere. I started to feel like I was walking around in circles, chasing something that was always just out of reach. I'd pour hours into tailoring my CV, rewriting my cover letter, adjusting everything to meet the job requirements. But it always felt like I was doing more work than the opportunity was worth.

I began to watch my peers, the ones who had entered the job market a few years before me. They were moving forward. They were getting hired. They were climbing the ladder one rung at a time, while I stood at the base, looking up, wondering why it was taking me so long to even take the first step. They had practical experience. They had spent years building their networks, gaining hands-on skills; meanwhile, here I was, fresh out of academia with nothing to offer but theory and research. It was maddening.

And the worst part? It wasn't even that I was jealous of their success. It was the constant reminder that I was being left behind. I had the knowledge. I had the qualifications. But the world didn't seem to care.

Every time I saw another friend or colleague post about their new job, the excitement in their eyes, the pride in their posts, I felt like I was sinking further into a pit of self-doubt. What was I doing wrong? Why wasn't I succeeding? Was my path always going to be different, harder than everyone else's?

It wasn't just that I felt stuck professionally—I felt stuck in my sense of self. I had spent so long building my identity around my academic achievements, but now that I was out in the real world, I had nothing to show for it. No title. No role. No tangible outcome for all of my hard work.

And that's the worst feeling of all—the feeling that everything you've worked for, everything you've sacrificed, might not matter. The feeling that your qualifications, your passion, your vision, aren't enough to change your reality.

I was caught in the paradox of being *overqualified* yet *under-experienced*, and the more I tried to fix it, the more I realized that the solution wasn't something I could apply for. It wasn't something that could be solved by filling out another job application, or by tweaking my resume. It was something deeper, something inside of me that I had to confront and reconcile before I could truly move forward.

The world had expectations for me. Society had expectations for me. And here I was, stuck—unable to meet them, unable to make sense of the very qualifications that should have set me free.

REFLECT AND RECONCILE

1. What expectations have you placed on your qualifications, and are they serving you?

   Reflect on how you've tied your worth to your achievements. Have you assumed that your degree or expertise would open doors automatically? What might happen if you reframed your qualifications as tools rather than guarantees?

2. How do you navigate being "too much" or "not enough"?

   The paradox of being overqualified yet under-experienced can feel defeating. How have you responded when the world's expectations seem contradictory? Are there ways to embrace this space as an opportunity for growth rather than a limitation?

3. What skills or experiences have you overlooked that could make you stand out?

   Sometimes we focus so much on what we lack that we miss what we already have. Look at your journey—your research, your passions, your ability to learn and adapt. What hidden strengths could you highlight to redefine how others see your value?

4. Are you trying to fit into a mold or break out of one?

   The job market often demands conformity, but true fulfilment often comes from carving out your own path. Are you bending yourself to fit someone else's expectations, or are you daring to create something uniquely yours?

5. What does progress look like when the first step feels unreachable?

   When doors don't open and opportunities seem distant, it's easy to feel stuck. What small, tangible actions can you take today—networking, learning new skills, or shifting your perspective—to move forward even when the path isn't clear?

Chapter 5

The Question That Changed Everything

WHO AM I?

It seems like such a simple question; one we answer without hesitation. Name. Job title. Profession. A neat little package of identity wrapped up and ready to present to the world. But what happens when you don't have a title anymore? What happens when the very things that defined you—student, researcher, nurse, academic—suddenly slip through your fingers, leaving you exposed, uncertain, and with nothing to hold onto?

I didn't realize how much of my identity was tied to my career until the rejections started piling up. At first, I held on to hope. After all, I had done everything right. I worked hard. I sacrificed. I stayed up through endless nights wrestling with data, refining arguments, pushing forward when exhaustion threatened to swallow me whole.

Applications sent. No response. Follow-ups written. Still nothing. Rejections, when they did come, were brief and impersonal—"We regret to inform you," "After careful consideration," "We appreciate your interest but have decided to move forward with another candidate." Over and over again. Each email felt like a chisel chipping away at the foundation of everything I thought I was.

At first, I told myself to be patient. Everyone struggles after graduation, right? It's just a matter of time. But as weeks stretched into months, and as those months turned into a year, something heavier settled over me: doubt. Fear. A creeping sense of inadequacy.

Had I overestimated my worth?

Had I wasted years of my life chasing a dream that was never meant to be mine?

It was a dangerous spiral, one I fought against every single day. But the thing about silence is that it doesn't just sit there. It grows. It echoes in your mind. It fills every space of your thoughts until you start to believe that maybe you were never meant to be heard in the first place.

The envelope felt heavier than it should have, as if it already knew what was inside. I sat at my desk—the same light, wood-color desk with natural, wood-grain pattern—that had been my station for years. The papers stacked haphazardly; a hot cup of herbal tea gone cold. Outside the window, the sky was a dull grey, the kind that blurred the time of day, making it feel like an endless stretch of waiting. I took a deep breath and tore open the envelope.

"We regret to inform you."

The words blurred together. Another rejection. Another door closed. Another polite but distant way of saying, *You're not good enough.*

I leaned back in my chair, rubbing my temples, exhaustion seeping into my bones. How many of these had I received now? Ten? Fifteen? More? I had lost count. Each one chipped away at something deep inside me, something I wasn't sure I could rebuild.

Paula walked in, her presence grounding me before she even spoke. She took one look at me and sighed.

"Another one?" she asked softly.

I nodded, not trusting myself to speak. She placed a hand on my shoulder, squeezing gently, the warmth of her touch reminding me that I wasn't alone.

"You'll get there," she said. "I know it."

I wanted to believe her. I wanted to hold onto her certainty when mine was slipping through my fingers.

Keanna, our daughter, was different. Yes, she was also proud of me—I knew that. She would always be my biggest cheerleader, but she was also living, moving forward in her own life, unburdened by the weight pressing down on me.

One evening, as we sat at the dinner table, she asked casually, "Dad, have you heard back from anywhere yet?"

I forced a smile. "Not yet."

She nodded while chewing her food. "You will." She said it with the kind of confidence only the young can have, as if success was inevitable.

I wanted to believe her too.

But the worst moments weren't at home. They were out in the world—unexpected casual conversations that twisted the knife.

I ran into an old colleague one afternoon at the supermarket. We exchanged pleasantries—and then came the question I dreaded: "So . . . what are you up to these days?"

I hesitated. Do I lie? Say I'm "exploring opportunities"? Make it sound like this was a choice? Instead, I forced a laugh: "Still looking. It's been a process."

They nodded, a flicker of awkwardness passing between us: "Well . . . I'm sure something will come up."

I smiled, but inside I was screaming.

That night I sat at my desk staring at my laptop screen. The question gnawed at me: *Who am I without my work?*

That thought terrified me because deep down I wasn't sure I liked the answer. My value had been tied so tightly to my job that without it I felt invisible, forgotten.

But in that moment . . . something shifted.

Instead of looking outward for validation, I began looking inward to ask myself, not about what I didn't have but about what I already had.

What was I doing right now that held meaning?

Where was I already making an impact?

And then . . . the answer came to me: the court; the community, the people who kept showing up every week finding something in that space they hadn't found anywhere else.

I had been searching for an opportunity without realizing I had already created one.

This realization didn't erase the struggles, but it reframed them.

For so long I had been waiting for someone else's permission to start my life; waiting for an employer's approval; waiting for external validation telling me I mattered.

But what if . . . .

What if I stopped waiting?

What if I stopped asking for permission?

What if the work meant for me—the work that truly mattered—was already right in front of me?

That was the moment Telford Community Basketball stopped being "just" a side project because it wasn't. It was something real, something alive, something with potential far greater than I'd ever imagined.

I wasn't lost or invisible anymore. And this time . . . .

I wasn't waiting for life to start because it already had.

REFLECT AND REDEFINE

1. What happens when your identity is no longer tied to what you do?

   If the roles and titles that have defined you were suddenly gone, who would you be? How can you begin to build a sense of self that isn't dependent on external labels but rooted in your values, passions, and inner worth?

2. Where are you already making an impact without realizing it?

   Sometimes the work that truly matters is happening quietly in the background of our lives. Look closely at your daily actions, your relationships, and the spaces where you show up for others. What are you contributing right now that holds meaning even if it isn't recognized by the world?

3. Are you waiting for permission to live fully?

   Think about the moments when you've hesitated, waiting for validation or approval before taking action. What would happen if you stopped waiting and trusted yourself to create something meaningful today?

4. How can you shift your focus from what's missing to what's already present?

   When life feels uncertain, it's easy to fixate on what we lack: opportunities, recognition, or progress. Take a moment to reflect on what's already in front of you. What strengths, relationships, or projects can you nurture to move forward with purpose?

5. What question could change everything for you right now?

   The question "Who am I?" led to a powerful realization in this chapter. What question are you avoiding in your own life, one that might unlock a new perspective or help you see your journey differently?

LEVEL C

The Unseen Opportunity

Basketball Was the Answer All Along

Theme: Purpose Is Already Present, We Just Have to See It

Chapter 6

A Court, a Community, a Calling

It started with a ball—just a ball. A simple, worn-out basketball, gripped by hands that carried the weight of stress, struggle, and survival. It started with a court—concrete, open, a space that didn't care about titles, degrees, or job applications. It started with a question, not one I asked out loud, but one that echoed deep inside me: *What if this could be more?*

But let's rewind. Let's go back to 2019, to the moment this all began, not as a movement, not as a structured initiative, not as something that I would one day call a calling. It started as an escape, a place to breathe, a way to move when the world felt stuck.

Basketball had always been there for me—long before the PhD, before the rejections, before the long nights staring at screens filled with unanswered emails. It was my first love, my therapy, my sanctuary. It didn't matter where life took me, how many obstacles I faced—whenever I stepped onto a court, something inside me unlocked. The world outside could be chaotic, overwhelming, unpredictable, but on the court, there was clarity, movement, freedom.

In 2019, when I first started gathering people to play, I wasn't thinking about building a community. I wasn't thinking about leadership or purpose. I just wanted a space where people—no matter their background, their struggles, their differences—could come together and just *play*. No judgment. No pressure. Just the sound of sneakers squeaking against the ground, the rhythm of the ball bouncing, the shared energy of movement, laughter, and release.

And that's exactly what happened.

People came. Not just people who were skilled or competitive, but those who had never picked up a ball in their lives. Some came for fitness, some for fun, others because they were looking for *something*—they just didn't know what. Week after week, the group grew. Different faces, different stories, different lives brought together by something as simple as a ball and a court.

But something strange started happening.

I noticed that it wasn't the game itself that kept people coming back. It wasn't about winning or losing, drills or strategy. It was the *atmosphere*—the feeling, the way we created a space where everyone belonged. There was no competition, just connection. There was no pressure to perform, just an invitation to be present, to show up, to move, to breathe, to exist in a space where, for a little while, the rest of life's worries faded into the background.

It was different. It was special. It was *bigger than basketball.*

And for the longest time, I didn't even realize what I had built.

Because back then, I was still measuring success the way the world had taught me to measure it: titles, salaries, recognized achievements. I was still chasing approval from the outside world, believing that only a certain kind of work mattered. I saw basketball as a *side thing*, something I did for fun, something separate from my "real" career.

But when I hit rock bottom—when job applications led to silence, when I started questioning my worth, when I found myself asking *Who am I without a job title?*—I finally saw it.

This wasn't just basketball.

This was community-building.

This was health.

This was social impact.

This was *leadership*.

What I had built wasn't just a casual gathering of players. It was something that mattered. It was a space where people, including myself, found *belonging* without needing permission, without needing to prove themselves. It was a space where people of all backgrounds, races, ages, and faiths came together, *not* to compete, but to lift each other up.

And maybe—just maybe—that was my real calling?

Maybe I wasn't supposed to wait for someone to hand me a position or a title. Maybe I wasn't meant to follow the traditional path, ticking boxes, waiting for the world to tell me I was enough. Maybe I had *already* created something meaningful, something impactful, something that had the power to grow into something *far bigger* than I had ever imagined.

The court had shown me something I couldn't ignore.

It wasn't just about playing basketball.

It was about giving people—myself included—a place to show up, to move, to belong.

And that? That was *everything.*

REFLECT AND DISCOVER

1. What spaces in your life have provided clarity and freedom?

   Think about the moments or places where you've felt truly free—free from judgment, pressure, or expectations. How can you create or nurture those spaces for yourself and others?

2. What simple actions have the potential to grow into something extraordinary?

   This chapter began with a ball and a court—two simple things that evolved into a community and a calling. What small, seemingly insignificant actions in your own life could hold the seeds of something greater?

3. How do you measure success in your life?

Are you still using the world's metric of titles, salaries, and recognition? Or have you started redefining success based on impact, connection, and belonging? What would it mean to embrace a new definition of success?

4. Who are you lifting up through your presence and actions?

   This chapter highlights the power of creating spaces where others feel seen and valued. Reflect on your own relationships. How are you showing up for others? How can you create more opportunities for connection and belonging in your community?

5. What calling might already be present in your life, but waiting for you to recognize it?

   Sometimes we search for purpose in far-off places, not realizing it's already within reach. Are there areas of your life—projects, passions, or relationships—that hold deeper meaning than you've acknowledged? How can you step fully into them?

Chapter 7

People Needed This and So Did I

AT FIRST, I THOUGHT I was just creating a space to play. A place for movement, for laughter, for stress relief. I never imagined that what started as a simple basketball gathering would grow into something that people *needed*. I never imagined it would become something that *I* needed just as much.

It wasn't until I heard their stories—the quiet confessions, the offhand remarks, the moments of transformation—that I understood the true weight of what we had built.

THE GIRL WHO FOUND HER VOICE

She barely spoke when she first arrived.

She was young—maybe nineteen or twenty years old—with long, dark hair that she kept tucked behind her ears. Her clothes were loose, almost too big for her frame, as if she was trying to disappear into them. Her sneakers were scuffed, and her hands fidgeted nervously with the hem of her hoodie. She stood off to the side of the court, watching but never stepping forward. Her shoulders were slightly hunched, her eyes downcast—the kind of posture that tried to make itself invisible.

I'd seen that look before. It was the look of someone who had spent years on the outside looking in, someone who wasn't sure if they belonged anywhere. She wasn't the only one like that; there were others who carried themselves with the same quiet hesitance. But something about her struck me—maybe it was how she lingered at the edge of the court, as if she wanted to join but couldn't quite bring herself to take that step.

When I encouraged her to join, she hesitated, shaking her head. "I don't really play," she said softly, her voice barely audible over the sound of bouncing basketballs and sneakers squeaking on the court.

"That's alright," I told her with a smile. "No pressure. Just have fun."

The first few sessions, she barely touched the ball. When it came her way, she'd pass it off quickly, almost reflexively, as if afraid of holding onto it for too long or drawing attention to herself. But week after week, she kept showing up. Something in the atmosphere must have made her feel safe enough to return.

And then, little by little, something changed.

One evening during a scrimmage game, she found herself with an open lane to the basket. For a brief moment, she froze—her eyes darting around as if waiting for someone else to take over—but then she dribbled past a defender and scored a layup. The ball swished cleanly through the net.

The group erupted in cheers.

It wasn't just polite clapping or casual encouragement. It was an explosion of noise: shouts of "Nice one!" and "Let's go!" filled the air. One guy even sprinted across the court to give her a high-five while others pounded their chests or clapped their hands in celebration. The sound echoed off the walls of the gym like a wave crashing over her.

And then . . . she smiled.

Not a small, polite smile—a real smile. It lit up her face in a way I hadn't seen before, like something inside her had shifted as if she had surprised even herself.

From that moment on, everything about her changed. She played harder. She spoke louder, calling for passes and directing teammates during games. She laughed more—a full-bodied laugh that seemed to come from somewhere deep within her—and it was contagious. She started taking up space on the court in ways that made it clear she wasn't afraid anymore.

Months later, after one particularly lively session where she had been unstoppable on defense, she pulled me aside as everyone else packed up their things.

"I used to be scared to even speak in a group," she admitted quietly, glancing down at her shoes before looking back up at me with a shy but genuine smile. "I've never felt like I belonged anywhere before. But here . . . here, I feel like I do."

Her words hit me hard, not just because of what they meant to her but because they made me realize something bigger: she wasn't alone in feeling that way.

This wasn't just basketball anymore—it was something much deeper than that. It was belonging. It was connection. It was transformation.

The court had become a place where people could show up exactly as they were—no pretenses, no expectations—and find something they didn't even know they were looking for: community.

And in creating this space for others . . . I realized I had found exactly what *I* needed too.

THE YOUNG MAN WHO USED TO RUN FROM THE LAW

Then there was him.

A young man in his early twenties, tall and lean, with a presence that carried both confidence and caution. His dark eyes held something heavy—an unspoken history—and his movements on the court were quick and deliberate, like someone who had learned to stay ahead of trouble. He didn't talk about his past much, but you could feel it trailing behind him like a shadow—a history with the law, bad choices, and the kind of reputation that makes doors shut before they even open.

And yet, here he was, on the same court, playing basketball with the very people he once saw as enemies: police officers.

At first, you could feel the tension. It wasn't overt or confrontational. It was subtle but unmistakable. The way his eyes flicked toward them when he thought no one was looking. The way he kept his distance during breaks, leaning against the wall with his arms crossed while others chatted freely. The way the officers exchanged glances when he joined in—a flicker of recognition passing between them.

But something about the game started to change things. It wasn't just basketball. It was the way we played it: without competition or judgment, just movement and connection. Slowly, the barriers began to dissolve.

One evening during a particularly intense session, he made a fast break down the court. His sneakers squeaked against the polished floor as he dodged defenders with ease. He passed the ball to one of the officers—a tall man with a commanding presence—and together they executed a perfect give-and-go play that ended with a clean shot through the hoop.

The sound of applause filled the gym—claps echoing off the walls alongside shouts of "Nice one!" and "That's teamwork!" Someone even whistled in approval. The young man turned toward his teammate—the officer—and gave him a quick nod before breaking into a grin that seemed to catch him off guard.

Later that night, as we packed up equipment and turned off lights, one of the officers pulled me aside. He nodded toward him—the young man now laughing with a group near the exit—and said quietly, "You know," he began, his voice tinged with both disbelief and pride, "I used to have to chase him down these streets. Every time I saw him, he was running. Now? He's here . . . laughing . . . playing . . . and for the first time, I think he actually sees us as human beings. Not just people who want to arrest him."

I let those words sink in because I had seen it too.

This young man—who once ran from the law—was now passing them the ball, strategizing with them during games, high-fiving them after good plays, and calling them "Bro" when they scored.

It wasn't about basketball anymore. It was about something much deeper than that.

For him—for all of us—the court had become more than just a place to play. It had become a space where labels didn't matter, where pasts didn't define futures, and where trust could be rebuilt one pass at a time.

This story added another layer to what we had created: a reminder that sometimes transformation doesn't come from lectures or programs or punishments—it comes from shared experiences in spaces where everyone feels equal.

And in creating this space for others . . . I realized I had found exactly what *I* needed too.

"I HAD NO COMMUNITY UNTIL I FOUND THIS"

One evening as we were packing up, a man in his late thirties lingered by the sidelines. He wasn't the most vocal player, but he showed up every week without fail.

"Can I tell you something?" he asked.

I nodded.

"I didn't have a community before this. No real friends, no place to go, nothing. I just went to work, went home, and that was it. But this? This is family, man."

I didn't know what to say at first.

Because how do you respond to something like that?

How do you respond when you realize that what you thought was just a casual meet-up was actually changing lives?

It was in that moment that I saw everything clearly.

I had been waiting—waiting for opportunities, waiting for someone to see my worth, to give me a job, to hand me a position that made me feel as if I was doing something *important.*

But the truth hit me hard—*I had already created something important.*

I didn't need permission.

I didn't need validation from some job title.

I had built a space where people found belonging, where they healed, where they connected, where their walls came down, and where *I* found purpose beyond the expectations that I had once placed on myself.

That night, as I looked around the court, I knew.

I wasn't just going to keep this going as a side project.

I was going *all in*.

No more waiting for permission. No more waiting for the world to tell me I was enough.

I had already created something powerful.

And now? It was time to own it.

REFLECT AND GROW

1. What is one step you can take today toward a more purposeful path?

   Change doesn't always come in grand gestures. It often begins with a single step. What is one small but intentional action you can take today to align your life more closely with your values and purpose?

2. How do your daily choices reflect the future you hope to create?

   Every decision, no matter how small, contributes to the bigger picture. Are your habits, priorities, and commitments leading you toward the life you envision? If not, what adjustments can you make?

3. Where in your life is action needed more than reflection?

   Reflection is valuable, but sometimes it becomes a substitute for action. Is there an area of your life where you've been waiting for the "right time" instead of moving forward? What would it look like to take a decisive step today?

4. Who can you partner with to create change?

Progress is rarely a solo journey. Who in your circle—or beyond—can help support and amplify the impact you hope to make? How can you reach out, collaborate, or invite others into your vision?

5. How will you hold yourself accountable for the actions you commit to?

   Intentions are powerful, but follow-through is what brings transformation. What systems, people, or reminders can help you stay on track with the commitments you make to yourself and your community?

LEVEL D

Building Something Bigger

Turning Passion into Legacy

Theme: Resilience, Action, Creating Impact on Your Own Terms

Chapter 8

No More Waiting—Making It Official

MARCH 17, 2025: THE day my mindset shifted forever.

For years I had been chasing recognition, waiting for someone to give me a title, a position, a reason to believe I was valuable. I had measured my worth through job offers that never came, through application portals that swallowed my CVs into silence. But, on that day, I stopped looking outward for validation because the truth hit me like a full-court sprint: *I had already built something worth fighting for.*

Telford Community Basketball wasn't just a side project. It wasn't just a few hours on the court each week, a way to pass the time while I searched for a "real" career. It was a movement. It was community-building at its core. It was impact, it was change, it was *purpose.* And yet, for so long, I had treated it as if it mattered only in the background of my life.

That ended on March 17, 2025—the day I made it official, the day I registered Telford Community Basketball as a Community Interest Company (CIC). No more waiting. No more hoping for permission. I was claiming the future on my own terms.

Filling out those registration forms wasn't just about legal status. It was a declaration. It meant that I was no longer just someone running a small initiative. I was a founder, a leader. I was someone responsible for something bigger than myself. It meant stepping up in ways I hadn't before: I was writing funding applications, creating sustainability plans, negotiating partnerships. It meant that if this failed, there was no one else to blame. There was no employer to fall back on, no organization to take the lead. It was terrifying. But it was also the most freeing decision I had ever made. I had spent so long waiting for a door to open on a house I didn't realize that *I had already built.*

I had to unlearn everything I thought success looked like. For years, I believed success meant landing a high-profile job, securing a prestigious role, climbing an institutional ladder. I had spent my life collecting degrees, awards, and accolades, convinced they were the stepping stones to a fulfilling career. But no matter how many applications I sent, no matter how many interviews I prepared for, nothing gave me the satisfaction I felt when I was on that basketball court, watching people come together, watching lives change through something as simple as community.

And I finally saw it: success wasn't something I had to chase. It was something I had already built. Telford Community Basketball had created a space for young people who needed it. It had given people a reason to show up, to belong, to connect. It had provided something schools, workplaces, and even local governments had struggled to offer: a sense of inclusion, a sense of purpose, a place where *everyone* mattered. And yet I had spent years treating it as a side note in my own life.

That had to change. If I wanted this to be more than just a passion project, I had to go all in. I had to stop treating it as something I did in between job applications and recognize it as the *work itself.* That meant making it sustainable. That meant treating it like the organization it was destined to be. That meant taking it as seriously as I had taken my PhD, my job search, my entire career. That meant building something that would outlast me.

I won't sugarcoat it—this part was hard. The moment I made the decision to turn Telford Community Basketball into an official organization, the weight of responsibility hit me like a brick wall. It wasn't just about showing up to the court anymore. It was about funding, legal structures, and long-term strategy. It was about convincing others to believe in a vision that, until now, had lived mostly in my head. And I had to admit that I wasn't fully prepared. I was stepping into unfamiliar territory. Writing grant proposals, learning financial structures, applying for funding—I had no formal training in any of it. I wasn't a businessperson. I wasn't an entrepreneur. I wasn't a CEO.

But that was the lie that I had been telling myself for too long. Because the truth was, I had *already* been leading. I had already built a thriving community from nothing. I had already been problem-solving, organizing, and fundraising even if it wasn't in the ways I had initially imagined. The world tells us leadership looks a certain way, that it comes with titles, boardrooms, suits, and a corner office. But I had been leading in a different way—on the court, in the conversations, in the way I made people feel when they walked into our sessions. And leadership doesn't need permission.

So, I leaned in. I studied. I learned everything I could about community funding, about social enterprises, about what it takes to run a CIC. I built partnerships. I spoke to local organizations, schools, funding bodies. I made it clear—this wasn't just about basketball. This was about *changing lives*. The work was exhausting, overwhelming at times. But the alternative—going back to waiting, hoping, relying on external validation—that was no longer an option. Because once you recognise your purpose, you can't unsee it.

There were moments of doubt, moments where I questioned if I was making a mistake, if I was putting all my energy into something that might not last. But then I'd step onto the court, and I'd see them: the young people who came every week, looking forward to the only space where they felt they truly belonged; the adults who joined, not just for exercise but for connection and escape from the stress of their lives; the strangers who had become teammates, friends, and family.

And I knew this wasn't just about me anymore. This wasn't about proving something to an employer, or making my CV look better, or even just finding a way to survive. This was about *them*.

This was about building something that could exist beyond me, something that would continue long after I was gone. This was about creating *legacy.*

So, I kept going. I filled out the paperwork. I made it official. I sought out funding, built partnerships, and leaned into the vision of what Telford Community Basketball could become. The work wasn't easy, but it was mine. And for the first time in a long time, I wasn't waiting for my life to begin.

I was *building* it—one decision, one step, one game at a time.

REFLECT AND COMMIT

1. What does taking ownership of your vision look like?

   Moving from an idea to an institution requires a shift in mindset. Where in your life can you take full responsibility for shaping your future instead of waiting for opportunities to appear?

2. What structures do you need to put in place for sustainability?

   Passion alone doesn't create longevity. What systems, resources, or partnerships could help turn your ideas into something lasting?

3. How do you embrace learning in unfamiliar territory?

   Stepping into a leadership role often means tackling areas where you have no formal training. How can you approach these challenges with curiosity rather than hesitation?

4. What sacrifices are necessary for the next stage of your journey?

   Every commitment comes with trade-offs. What are you willing to let go of to make space for what truly matters?

5. How will you measure the impact of what you're building?

Beyond personal growth, how will you track the difference your work is making in the lives of others? What will success look like five years from now?

Chapter 9

The Power of Saying Yes to Yourself

The truth is, life rarely unfolds the way we expect. We make plans, map out the future, chase after dreams, but more often than not, the path twists, turns, and sometimes, it seems to vanish entirely beneath our feet.

I had spent years working toward my PhD, pouring myself into every page, every hour of research, believing that at the end of it, a door would swing open. The world would welcome me in. The letters after my name would mean something, not just academically but in the way that opportunities would appear, invitations would come, and suddenly, I'd be standing in the room where I belonged.

But when the final chapter was written and the cap thrown into the air, reality struck like a cold wind.

No matter how many applications I sent, no matter how carefully I crafted my cover letters, the answer was always the same: silence; or worse, rejection.

I would sit at my desk late into the night, my laptop screen casting an eerie blue glow against the dim walls, my inbox full of echoes of disappointment. The polite phrasing of rejection emails always felt the same. *We regret to inform you. We had a competitive pool of applicants. We wish you the best in your future endeavors.*

It was like an infinite loop of doors closing, one after another, each one slamming shut just as I dared to hope.

At first, I told myself it was temporary, a rough patch, just another test of endurance. I had worked hard before. I had pushed through challenges, overcome barriers. This was just another one, right?

But months passed. Applications turned into dozens, then hundreds. Each one meticulously prepared, carefully worded, tailored to fit the role. And yet, rejection followed rejection.

Doubt crept in like a slow-moving fog, thick and suffocating. *Maybe I'm not good enough. Maybe I overestimated my worth. Maybe all the years I spent—sleepless nights hunched over my desk, hours dissecting theories and analyzing data—were for nothing.*

I had convinced myself that if I just worked hard enough, if I just *wanted* it badly enough, success would come. That's what we are told, isn't it? Perseverance wins. Effort is always rewarded.

But the world doesn't work that way.

It isn't about effort alone. It isn't about passion alone. It isn't even about talent alone. And that realization cut deep.

I found myself questioning everything. *Was I supposed to succeed? Had I missed something vital that others seemed to grasp so easily?* I watched as peers moved effortlessly into new roles, their LinkedIn announcements shining like beacons of achievement. Meanwhile, I was stuck, trapped in an endless cycle of trying and failing.

I didn't tell anyone how much it was eating at me. It's one thing to speak of rejection when it's occasional, when it's a lesson to be learned. But when rejection becomes your reality, when it begins to shape the way you see yourself, you stop talking about it. You pretend it isn't happening because admitting it out loud makes it feel too real.

I prayed, desperately.

I asked God for clarity, for an open door, for even the smallest sign that I was not simply wandering aimlessly. I begged him to show me where I was meant to be. But heaven was silent.

And in that silence, I made a decision.

If doors wouldn't open, I would keep knocking. If opportunities weren't appearing, I would create my own.

But first, I had to let go of the idea that success had to look a certain way.

I had been so fixated on a job title defining my worth that I had failed to see what was already in front of me.

Telford Community Basketball wasn't just a hobby. It wasn't just a way to pass the time between job applications. It was *alive.* It was breathing, growing, impacting lives in ways I had never fully acknowledged.

Every practice, every game, every conversation was a ripple effect, reaching further than I had imagined. Young people who had felt invisible were finding confidence. Strangers were becoming teammates, then friends, then a family. The game was doing what institutions had failed to do: bringing people together, lifting them up, giving them purpose.

And somewhere in that I realized that *I had been waiting for a door to open when I had already built a house.*

God had been guiding me all along, not through loud proclamations or obvious signs but through the steady unfolding of events, through the disappointments that nudged me toward something greater. I had prayed for direction, begged for an open door, but he had already placed me where I needed to be. I just hadn't recognized it yet.

And so I did something radical. I stopped chasing.

I stopped seeing rejection as a verdict on my worth. I stopped measuring success by the world's standards. I stopped searching for permission to step into the space I had already created for myself.

Instead, I leaned in.

I poured my energy into what I had built, into the work that was already making an impact. And slowly, things began to shift, not in the way I had originally imagined, not in the way I had once hoped, but in a way that was deeper, richer, and more real.

Opportunities that had once felt so distant began to appear, not because I had chased them but because I had become ready for them.

It wasn't instant. It wasn't easy. But I finally understood: success was never about climbing a corporate ladder. It was about impact. And I was already making one.

So to anyone feeling stuck, to anyone staring at rejection after rejection, I need you to hear this: *your purpose isn't lost; it's waiting for you to recognize it.*

We spend so much time searching for meaning outside of ourselves, believing that fulfilment is something we have to *find.* But sometimes, it's already within us. It's woven into everything we've done, every passion we've pursued, every small step we've taken without realizing its significance.

Saying yes to yourself isn't about arrogance. It's about faith.

It's about faith in the journey you've walked, faith in the purpose that has been growing within you, faith that even when doors close, God is still leading you exactly where you need to be.

So stop waiting. Stop seeking permission. Step forward in faith and take the next step. Because sometimes, the life you're meant to live is the one that's been unfolding all along. You just have to open your eyes to see it.

REFLECTION AND FAITH

1. Trusting God's Quiet Guidance

   This journey has shown me that God often works in ways I don't immediately recognize. I prayed for clarity, for open doors, and for direction, but heaven seemed silent. Yet, looking back, I can see that God had been guiding me all along, not through dramatic signs, but through the steady unfolding of events and the work I was already doing. Faith isn't always about hearing loud answers. It's about trusting that God is leading me even when the path feels unclear. Are you willing to trust that God's plan is unfolding in your life, even if you can't see it yet?

2. Rejection as Divine Redirection

Rejection once felt like a crushing blow, but I now see it as part of God's greater plan. Every closed door was a nudge toward something better, toward a purpose that aligns more deeply with my gifts and calling. When I faced rejection, I reminded myself that God's "no" was often a "not yet" or a "this isn't for you." Instead of resisting, I leaned into faith, trusting that every disappointment was redirecting me toward something greater. How can you lean into faith and trust that every disappointment is redirecting you toward something greater?

3. Recognizing the Blessings I Already Have

   I spent so much time chasing external success that I failed to see the blessing God had already placed in my hands: Telford Community Basketball. It wasn't until I stopped searching outward that I realized my purpose had been growing right in front of me all along. Faith calls me to open my eyes to the blessings I already have instead of constantly seeking more. What has God already given you that you might be overlooking? How can you honor and invest in those blessings?

4. Saying Yes to God's Plan for Me

   Saying yes to myself isn't just about self-confidence. It's about saying yes to the purpose God has placed within me. I stopped measuring success by worldly standards and started embracing the work that God had been quietly preparing me for. Faith invites me to trust that I am enough because I am created for a unique purpose. Are you ready to stop chasing what the world says you should want and start embracing what God has already prepared for you?

5. Faith in the Journey, Not Just the Destination

   This chapter of my life reminds me that faith is not just about believing in the outcome. It's about trusting the source and the journey itself. Even when doors closed and rejection felt endless, God was still working behind the scenes, shaping my path and preparing my heart for what was ahead. I learned to lean into my faith and let go of the need for control, trusting that God was leading me exactly where I needed to be. How can you surrender your plans to God and trust him with each step of your journey?

LEVEL E

Living It Out

Becoming the Purpose

Theme: Embodiment, Legacy in Motion, Leading from Who You Are

Chapter 10

You Are the Platform Now

What I did not realize at the beginning of this journey was that I was not just preparing for a role. I was forming for something much greater. It wasn't simply about writing a thesis or starting a basketball initiative or weathering the storm of unanswered applications. It was about becoming someone who could carry a message, who could hold space for others, and who could stand firm in their own skin when nothing around them seemed to make sense.

And here is what I have come to know for certain: you are the platform. You're not the job; not the stage; not the title or invitation.

When I finally stopped waiting to be chosen and instead chose myself, I began to operate from a different place. It was not arrogance. It was authority, rooted in knowing who I was, who I am. That kind of knowing changes everything.

Let me tell you about a moment I will never forget. I was sitting in my small home office in Telford. The light was dim, and it was one of those grey English afternoons where the sky seems to press down on your shoulders. I had just received another rejection email. This was from an organization I had really wanted to work for, one whose values seemed to mirror mine. I had crafted that application with care. I had imagined myself in the role. I had already pictured how I would walk into that building, contribute to their mission, and feel a sense of arrival. But the email said otherwise.

I sat there in silence for a long time. My laptop was still open. The cursor blinked like it was taunting me. And then, almost as a reflex, I opened the folder marked "Basketball Project—Community Files." Inside were photos from recent sessions, feedback from participants, notes I had written after court conversations about someone's confidence growing, or a young person speaking up for the first time, or a mother who told me, "My son has something to look forward to now."

At that moment, something changed. I realized that I was already doing the thing I had been waiting to be hired to do. I was already in motion; already building impact; already walking with purpose. I was the platform.

This doesn't mean I didn't still want structure, support, or financial security—of course I did. Of course I *do*. But I stopped waiting for them to validate what I already knew deep down: that I had something to offer; that my lived experience, my resilience, and my passion were enough to begin.

And you do too.

You don't need to have it all figured out. You don't need every piece in place. You just need to recognize what's already within you. The platform you're waiting for might be the one you're meant to create.

Creating your own platform is not easy. It comes with risk. It comes with sacrifice. It comes with the uncertainty of not knowing how others will respond or if anyone will show up. But do it anyway; build anyway; begin anyway. Because there is someone waiting on the other side of your courage.

And I'll tell you this: there's a kind of joy that comes when you start to live in alignment; when your values match your actions; when your gifts get exercised instead of shelved; when your voice—trembling or not—starts to echo because you dared to use it.

You begin to feel alive, alive in the truest sense; not busy, not merely productive, but aligned. There's peace in that place. There's strength in it. There's energy that doesn't burn out easily because it's fed by meaning, not by striving.

Let me make this practical. If you're building something—be it a book, a community project, a creative piece, a mentoring group—treat it with the same seriousness you would if someone hired you to do it. Show up. Stay accountable. Keep learning. Keep refining. Speak about it with confidence, not apology.

Too many people wait until someone "important" notices them. But I've learned that significance starts in the shadows. Purpose grows quietly before it ever gets a spotlight. The impact you're hoping to make—it's being forged now, in private, in persistence, in quiet faithfulness.

And I want to say something else, especially if you're someone of faith: there's something sacred about becoming the platform. It means you've become a vessel, one that carries a message bigger than yourself. It means you're no longer just telling your story; you're telling the story that others see themselves inside. And when that happens, healing begins; doors open; chains fall. People breathe deeper because they've encountered something real.

This is not about ego. It's about legacy. Legacy isn't built when the world claps. Legacy is built when you decide to stay the course, when you keep showing up even when the room is half empty or the results are slow. It's built in your integrity. It's built when you do the right thing when no one's watching. It's built when you answer your call, even when you feel unequipped.

You are equipped; maybe not perfectly but enough to begin.

That's what I want this chapter to be for you: a beginning. I want it to be the moment where you stop asking "Who will choose me?" and start declaring, "I choose me." I want it to be the moment where you stop shrinking to fit the room and start standing in the fullness of your purpose. I want it to be the moment where you stop asking for a seat at someone else's table and realize you've been building one all along.

You are the platform now. Stand tall. Speak truth. Start.

REFLECT AND SURRENDER

1. What am I still waiting to be validated by, when I already know I've been called?

   It's easy to crave recognition from others; to want the title, the salary, the invitation that tells us we're worthy. But when you've already been called, the need for outside validation loses its power. You were chosen before you were acknowledged. Trust that truth, and move accordingly.

2. Where am I striving for visibility instead of trusting in quiet obedience?

   There's a difference between showing up boldly and striving desperately. One flows from purpose, the other from pressure. If the spotlight is the goal, we'll miss the richness of growth in the shadows. Trust that what's being built in silence will one day speak loudly.

3. What platform am I being invited to build with what's already in my hands?

   Look around. What conversations, ideas, passions, or tools are already within your reach? You don't need a grand blueprint to start. Purpose often begins with what's close and familiar. Honor what's already in your hands; it may be the seed of your next movement.

4. What does surrender look like in this season? Is it not giving up but letting go of control?

   Surrender doesn't mean quitting. It means loosening your grip on how things must unfold. It means trusting that the process, with all its detours and delays, is shaping something in you. Let go of forcing outcomes. Embrace the peace of faithful presence.

5. How can I shift my energy from proving to becoming?

Proving yourself is exhausting. Becoming yourself is liberating. Let your work, your words, and your presence rise from a place of truth, not tension. You're not here to impress. You're here to embody. Let your focus be wholeness, not performance.

Reflect. Surrender. Trust. Repeat.

Because that is how platforms become movements. That is how purpose becomes legacy.

Chapter 11

Legacy in Motion

Legacy isn't something you leave behind one day in the distant future. It's something you live, breathe, and build with every choice, every conversation, every moment of faithfulness today. After the awakening of chapter 10—realizing that you are the platform—comes the quieter, humbler, but equally sacred task of *walking it out*; living it out; becoming the message.

You don't need a podium to influence lives. You don't need a spotlight to start a legacy. The most impactful legacies are often built in quiet spaces, in consistent decisions that may never trend but will transform. That's where I found myself, not in headlines or accolades but in the simplicity of being available, present, and faithful to what I had.

It was the morning after a community basketball session. Nothing particularly grand had happened. We played, we talked, someone new joined, and someone else lingered after everyone had left. That's when I heard it, a quiet, almost casual voice saying, "Thanks, I needed this today." And in that moment, I remembered: *legacy doesn't announce itself; it whispers.*

Legacy is motion. It's not stagnant or ceremonial. It flows. It changes shape as you keep showing up. For me, legacy became real when I stopped trying to plan it and started embodying it. When

I stopped asking "What do I want to be remembered for?" and started living in a way that naturally answered the question.

It's the consistent showing up that carves the path of legacy. The way you treat the person no one notices. The grace you extend when no one sees. The courage to keep building something that others can stand on, even if they never know your name.

Legacy in motion is mentorship without fanfare. It's lifting others while you're still learning. It's believing in someone else's gift before they can see it. It's that moment you follow up, send a message, make space—the work no one claps for, but heaven notices.

And let me be honest: it's not always inspiring. Sometimes, it's exhausting. Sometimes you give and wonder if it's making any difference. You sow, and it feels like nothing grows. You pour out, and you're met with silence. But this is where legacy is most refined: in the unseen, unrewarded moments of obedience.

There were seasons I questioned it all, when I felt overlooked, when I wondered if I had missed the path entirely. But in those seasons, I learned that legacy isn't about outcome. It's about alignment. It's about doing what you're called to do, not what you're applauded for.

I began to realize that people weren't just listening to what I taught. They were watching what I tolerated, how I responded, how I treated others, how I endured difficulty. And slowly, something beautiful happened: I became the message; not a perfect messenger, but a living letter.

If you're wondering what your legacy is, don't look for monuments. Look at your habits. Look at your relationships. Look at the people who feel seen, empowered, and inspired because of your presence.

We often think legacy means something massive, something lasting in physical terms. But I've come to believe that the most eternal legacies are relational, not built in bricks but in people.

You may never know how your kindness kept someone from giving up, how your encouragement helped someone believe again, how your faithfulness created stability in someone's chaos. But trust me, legacy is in motion.

Here's what I know now: living out your purpose will not always feel groundbreaking. It might feel ordinary. It might feel repetitive. But that's where the gold is. Legacy is often disguised as routine. It hides in consistency. It matures in surrender.

I had to let go of the idea that purpose always feels purposeful. Sometimes it feels like just showing up tired, like listening when you'd rather speak, like praying when the answers feel delayed, or like investing in others when no one is investing in you.

But in all those quiet motions, something is being built; something generational, something eternal.

Legacy in motion also means growing with your purpose. It means letting your vision evolve. What began for me as a basketball session became a space for healing, unity, and unexpected leadership development. Over time, I realized that legacy wasn't just what I was doing, it was what others were becoming because of what I was doing.

I've seen young people step up to mentor others. I've seen adults reconnect with joy, confidence, and belonging. I've seen bridges built between people who would never have crossed paths otherwise. All of that? Legacy in motion.

And here's the thing: it multiplies. When you live your purpose openly and consistently, others catch the vision. They begin to ask, "What could I do? What's in my hand?" And before you know it, what started as one person's faith becomes a movement of faithfulness.

So I want to encourage you. If you're in a season where nothing feels big or bold or noticeable, don't underestimate the power of your "yes"—your "yes" to staying; your "yes" to building; your "yes" to believing again; your "yes" to planting seeds without demanding to see the harvest tomorrow.

Your daily "yes" *is* legacy in motion.

Keep going.

Live it.

Be it.

And when you doubt your impact, pause and ask, "What fruit might be growing that I haven't yet seen?" Because in the kingdom of legacy, things often grow deep before they grow visible.

You don't have to force legacy; just keep walking.

Keep loving.

Keep showing up.

REFLECTION AND RELEASE

1. Legacy is lived, not left

   Legacy isn't a future event or a plaque on a wall. It's the impact of your daily faithfulness. It's how you treat people when no one is watching. It's built in the choices you make, the integrity you walk in, and the love you consistently give. You don't build legacy one day; you live it today.

2. Influence happens in unseen moments

   Some of your most impactful moments may never be posted or praised. True influence happens in the background, in your phone calls, follow-ups, the time you gave when it wasn't convenient. The unseen moments are often the soil of transformation for someone else's breakthrough.

3. You become the message

   The world watches how you carry what you believe. When your actions align with your values, you become a walking testimony. You don't have to be loud to be powerful; you just need to be consistent. Becoming the message means you live with enough authenticity that your life speaks louder than your words.

4. Relational legacy is the most lasting

   Titles fade and platforms shift, but relationships endure. The way you empower others, listen deeply, and create safe space leaves a mark that outlives you. Your legacy is not what you built alone, but what others became because you walked beside them.

5. Your daily "yes" creates generational momentum

   Purpose isn't always loud, but it is cumulative. Every small act of obedience compounds into something significant over time. What feels like routine today could become the very foundation someone else stands on tomorrow. Say yes to your purpose and trust that your "yes" echoes far beyond your lifetime.

LEVEL F

The Ripple Effect

Purpose That Multiplies

Theme: Expansion, Multiplication, and Commissioning

Chapter 12

The Echo of Your "Yes"

IT STARTS WITH A whisper, a stirring, a sense that something is asking to be answered inside of you. For me, that whisper didn't come from a stage or a headline. It came in the quiet, in the space between rejection and realization. I had been waiting for someone to open a door, but the invitation had been inside me all along.

When you say "yes" to your purpose, you're not just answering for yourself. You're echoing something that gives others permission to say "yes" too. That's the sacred ripple of courage—it multiplies. It travels farther than you will ever see. Your "yes" becomes an echo in someone else's silence, a spark in their fog, a light on their horizon.

I didn't know what would come from starting a noncompetitive basketball initiative. It seemed so simple. It was a way to gather, to offer something safe and consistent. But over time, I saw what I couldn't have planned. Young people walked in unsure and walked out with lifted heads. Adults rediscovered joy and identity. Police officers found common ground with those they once arrested. Conversations replaced conflict. Community replaced isolation. And all this because of one "yes," one choice to act, even when I didn't have the full picture.

Your "yes" doesn't need to be loud to be powerful. It needs to be genuine. It needs to be rooted in something real. Because when your "yes" comes from alignment with who you are, it carries authority. And that kind of authority doesn't shout—it resonates. It stays. It lingers in the room long after you leave.

There are people you may never meet whose lives are impacted by your willingness to be obedient to a quiet prompting. That's the part we often forget: purpose isn't always visible. Sometimes it's invisible seeds taking root. Sometimes it's legacy whispering through your faithfulness. And sometimes it's another person finding the strength to step forward because they saw you do it first.

I once received a message from someone who had attended just one basketball session. I barely remembered the conversation we had. But they wrote, "I saw something in how you listened. It made me want to speak up for the first time in months." That was it. One moment, one presence, and something changed, not because I gave a speech but because I showed up.

This is what the echo of your "yes" looks like. It lives in the ripple. It lives in the story that continues without you having to be the center of it. It lives in the lives changed because you said "yes" to being available, to being faithful, to being real.

And let me say this clearly: the echo doesn't need you to be perfect. It needs you to be present. You don't need to have all the answers. You don't need to carry the weight of everyone's transformation. You just need to carry your piece with integrity, with love, with consistency.

That's what multiplies; that's what makes movements. It's not noise but depth; not image but impact; not hype but heart.

Your "yes" is a seed. And seeds don't just feed one tree—they start forests.

So if you're wondering whether your "yes" matters, I'm here to tell you it does; more than you know. And someone, somewhere, is waiting to echo it back.

But I want to take you deeper into this. Because I know what it feels like to say "yes" and then wonder if anyone heard it, to take the leap and find yourself mid-air, unsure if the net exists at all. Your "yes" might not be met with applause. It might be met with resistance, confusion, or even loneliness. But that doesn't make it wrong. It makes it real.

There was a time I stood in an empty gym. I had arrived early for a basketball session, but no one else had shown up yet. The lights buzzed overhead. The court was quiet. For a moment, I questioned everything. Was this worth it? Was I really making a difference? Should I just pack up and leave?

But something told me to stay. And ten minutes later, one participant walked in. Then another. Then two more. And that night, something happened on the court: a conversation that opened a door for healing, a breakthrough in someone who had been silent for months, and I thought to myself, "What if I had left?"

Sometimes the echo of your "yes" shows up late. But it always arrives.

Purpose isn't about immediate results. It's about sustained obedience. It's about showing up with hope when evidence hasn't yet caught up. And it's about trusting that your small yes might be the domino that sets a greater story into motion.

The most profound echoes often come from the "yeses" that were least convenient. The ones that demanded humility. The ones that asked you to sacrifice your comfort for someone else's breakthrough. That's the beauty of real purpose—it expands you while freeing others.

I remember speaking to a young man who had been on the fringes. For weeks he would come late, sit off to the side, and rarely engage. Then one day, I caught him lingering after a session. We ended up talking for nearly an hour. He told me, "I've never had anyone stay after just for me." That wasn't part of the plan. It wasn't an event or a strategy. It was a moment, a simple "yes" to connection. And it changed something in him. He became one of our most consistent attendees, even bringing others along with him.

You never know what someone else's turning point will be. But if you're willing to be available, your yes will become the echo that gets them there.

We often wait for perfect conditions, for clarity, for a guaranteed return. But purpose doesn't usually come with blueprints. It comes with nudges. And when you honor those nudges, when you lean in and say, "Yes, I'll go," the path begins to shape itself.

Don't despise the size of your "yes." Don't discount it because it feels ordinary. Your "yes" may be the only light someone sees that day. Your smile, your text, your presence in a room—it might carry the weight of a divine appointment.

And don't be surprised when your "yes" comes full circle, when someone who once watched from a distance steps into their own boldness because they saw you walk in yours. That's how purpose multiplies. That's how movements begin, not with a megaphone but with a whisper, a whisper answered with a "yes."

Let your "yes" be rooted in love, not fear; in clarity of values, not clarity of outcome; in the conviction that purpose isn't about grandeur, it's about grace. And as you say "yes," over and over again, watch how others begin to rise, echoing back the same courage you once had to summon on your own.

Because courage is contagious.

And your "yes"—it's more powerful than you think.

Shall we keep going with the next section?

REFLECTION AND RESONANCE

1. Where has my "yes" already created ripples I may not fully see?

   Take time to think about where you've shown up, even in uncertainty. Who might have been watching? Who might have found courage because you dared to act in quiet faithfulness? Sometimes your echo is unfolding in places you haven't even stepped into yet.

2. What kind of "yes" is rising in me now but waiting for my permission to move?

   Often, we sense what we're being asked to do long before we act. What is your spirit whispering? What is waiting to be released through your decision to show up again with more boldness, more presence, more vulnerability?

3. Who has echoed courage back to me, and how can I honor them?

   We're all shaped by the "yeses" of others. Take a moment to name someone whose courage helped call yours forth. Then ask: How can I be that echo for someone else?

4. Am I withholding my "yes" because I fear it won't be enough?

   There is no such thing as a small "yes" when it comes to purpose. Every time you say "yes" to alignment, you break a little more ground. What would shift if you trusted that your obedience, not your outcome, is what truly matters?

5. What space can I create for others to echo their "yes"?

   Legacy doesn't end with us, it multiplies through us. How are you building platforms, inviting voices, or holding space for others to rise? Your "yes" may be the spark that ignites someone else's beginning.

Chapter 13

Leave the Door Open

It would be tempting to think the story ends when you find your voice, step into your purpose, and begin to walk in your calling. But real purpose doesn't close doors, it opens them. And legacy doesn't stop at personal fulfilment. Legacy invites others in.

I've come to believe that the most powerful people aren't the ones who race ahead alone. They're the ones who slow down just enough to bring others with them. They're not just climbing, they're carrying. They're not just building, they're making room. This is what it means to leave the door open.

When I began Telford Community Basketball, I didn't fully grasp what I was creating. At first, it was just a space, something small, consistent, healing. But over time, I started to realize something much bigger was happening. This wasn't just about sport or sessions. It was about trust. It was about transformation. It was about belonging.

And most of all, it was about making sure others felt welcome.

There's something holy about hospitality, not the kind where you have to dress it up but the kind that says, "Come as you are. There's space for you here." I began to notice that what people remembered most wasn't the activity, it was how they were received. It was the smile at the door, the listening ear, the sense that they weren't being evaluated or compared but accepted.

That's the kind of door I want to leave open.

I want to be someone who doesn't just find a way through. I want to make a way. I want my "yes" to create space for others' "yeses." I want my breakthroughs to break chains for the people behind me.

There's a myth that purpose is scarce, that if you rise, someone else has to fall. But true purpose is abundant. It multiplies. And when you share what you've learned—when you speak up, open doors, hold space, and tell your story—you're not diminishing your power. You're passing it on.

I've seen this firsthand. I've watched shy teenagers become confident young leaders, not because I gave them a lecture but because I gave them a chance. I've seen people return to sessions not because of a program but because they felt seen. I've watched relationships form between strangers who might have never crossed paths if not for that open door.

One of the most memorable moments came when a young woman who had barely spoken in her first few months stood up and offered to colead a group. Her voice trembled at first, but her presence was strong. She told me later, "I just needed someone to believe I had something to say."

That's the fruit of an open door.

Leaving the door open means believing there's room for more—more voices, more growth, more change. It means you stop hoarding wisdom and start planting seeds. It means mentoring, sharing, including, inviting. It means not being threatened by the next generation, but preparing the ground for them.

When I look at the world around me, I see so many people waiting outside doors; waiting to be noticed, to be invited, to be given permission. But what if we stopped waiting for gatekeepers and started becoming gateways?

What if your story became someone else's signpost?

What if your scar became someone else's survival guide?

What if your platform became a porch—wide, welcoming, and strong enough to hold more than just you?

Leaving the door open requires humility. It requires a shift from success to significance, from arrival to accessibility, from "I've made it" to "We're making it."

There's no greater honor than being a builder of bridges, a holder of keys, a door-leaver-opener. Because it means your life is no longer just about you. It's about impact. It's about multiplication. It's about generational momentum.

So as you walk in your purpose, don't forget to look back.

Who's behind you?

Who's watching?

Who's waiting for an invitation you're equipped to give?

Your story isn't just a victory, it's a road map. Your struggle isn't just a scar, it's a signal. Your faithfulness isn't just personal, it's powerful.

Leave the door open.

Let your life say, "There's room for you too."

Let your example speak louder than your title.

Let your legacy be more than what you built; let it be who you built up.

Because in the end, greatness isn't about who knows your name. It's about how many people you made space for. And the world is waiting for that kind of greatness.

When you become the door, you don't control who walks through; you welcome them. You don't get to choose their background, their wounds, or their readiness. But you choose to see them. You choose to make room. And you trust that something sacred happens when people feel safe enough to belong.

This is how we lead now, not by building walls of status or exclusivity but by building long tables and wide porches. This is how movements expand, not with a megaphone but with a message lived so boldly that others begin to see their own story inside it.

Leaving the door open isn't a leadership strategy. It's a posture of the heart. It's the difference between empire-building and community-building. It's the choice to pursue influence, not for applause but for access—access to possibility, to healing, to purpose.

It means choosing to be interruptible. It means not seeing people as a threat to your journey, but as co-travellers. It means not needing credit to be content.

And it means trusting that your legacy is most alive when it is being carried by others.

So pause right here and ask yourself the following questions:

- Who have I made space for lately?
- Who needs an invitation I've been too busy or afraid to extend?
- Who's watching me model what's possible, and what do I want them to see?

This isn't about being perfect. It's about being present. Open doors don't require polished speeches. They require willingness. And sometimes, they just require showing up one more time than you felt like it.

That's what I want my life to echo: not just success but shared success, not just purpose fulfilled but purpose passed on.

So whatever you're building—whether it's a community, a classroom, a ministry, a book, or a business—build it with others in mind. Build it so someone can follow. Build it so they can go further. Build it so no one has to ask, "Am I allowed to be here?"

Let your open door be an answer before the question is even spoken. Because when you leave the door open, you don't just change someone's moment. You just might change their life.

REFLECTION AND INVITATION

1. Where have I already made space for someone and how did it feel?

   Take a moment to remember a time when you invited someone in, supported a new voice, or created room for another to grow. Reflect on how that decision impacted not just them but you. Our purpose often expands when we make space for others.

2. What does "leaving the door open" look like in my life right now?

   Leaving the door open doesn't have to be dramatic. It can be as simple as a conversation, a recommendation, or an encouragement. Identify one area—your workplace, your home, your community—where someone might be waiting for an opening you can create.

3. Who has left a door open for me and how can I honor that gift?

   None of us arrived where we are alone. Think about the mentors, encouragers, or quiet champions who made space for you. How might you carry their legacy forward by doing the same for someone else?

4. Where have I been tempted to close the door out of fear or scarcity?

   It's human to want to protect what we've built. But what might shift if you viewed your platform as a shared space rather than a pedestal? Legacy multiplies when it is released, not restricted.

5. What invitation can I offer this week?

   An invitation could be spoken, written, or felt. Who needs to hear "There's room for you here"? Don't wait for the perfect moment—extend the welcome. Your invitation might be the answer to someone's silent question.

Up Next: The Twenty-One-Day Purpose Challenge

If the last chapter stirred something in you, the next part of this book is your invitation to keep walking. What follows is "From PhD To Purpose: The Twenty-One-Day Purpose Challenge"—a guided journey of daily reflections and small actions designed to help you say yes to yourself, build momentum, and keep your purpose alive.

Whether you're stepping out for the first time or stepping back into your calling with new clarity, this challenge is your next step forward.

Let's continue together.

Before you launch into the "Twenty-One-Day Purpose Challenge," pause and take in what this moment truly means. You're not just turning the page, you're stepping into possibility, into courage, into a space where purpose doesn't stay a concept but becomes a practice.

This challenge is your next step, not because you need to prove anything but because you've already proven one powerful truth: you're ready to show up for yourself, ready to move forward with clarity, conviction, and compassion.

You won't need hours of free time or a perfect environment. You'll just need ten to fifteen intentional minutes a day. You'll need a journal, an open heart, and a willingness to be honest. Each day, you'll receive a reflection, a prompt, and an action. Together, they form a rhythm, a daily return to purpose.

And if you miss a day, don't quit. Real transformation isn't linear. Return to the page, take a breath, and pick up where you left off. That's not failure, that's faithfulness.

This isn't about being perfect. It's about being present. It's about choosing to walk out what you've already begun to believe: that your life matters, your story counts, and your purpose is unfolding.

So let this be your moment.

Let this be your line in the sand.

Let this be the day you say—clearly, unapologetically, and without delay—"I'm ready."

Because the next twenty-one days aren't just a challenge.

They're an awakening.

And if at any point along the way you feel like you can't carry on, then pause, don't quit. Remember that purpose is not built in perfection but in persistence. You don't have to feel ready to take the next step, you just have to be willing. Even a trembling "yes" carries power. Even a whisper of hope can move mountains. The fact that you're still here, still curious, still reaching—that's proof enough that you're capable of continuing. This journey is not about never falling, it's about refusing to stay down.

So, then, because we only have this present moment, let's begin.

Final Thoughts

You Already Have What You Need

- Life doesn't always go as planned, but sometimes the detour leads to your real purpose
- Resilience isn't just about enduring, it's about seeing what's in front of you differently
- You don't need a spotlight to make an impact—your presence, your kindness, and your courage are already changing lives
- Purpose doesn't ask for perfection—it asks for participation, for movement, for showing up
- The journey you're on may be messy, but it's meaningful; every step forward is proof that you're building something real
- There's no one else who can carry your story the way you can—your voice matters more than you know

Stop waiting for doors to open. Build your own!

From PhD to Purpose

Twenty-One-Day Purpose Challenge

Daily Reflections and Actions to Say "Yes" to Yourself and Build a Life of Impact

WELCOME TO THE CHALLENGE

Congratulations on choosing to show up for yourself. This twenty-one-day challenge is designed to help you discover, affirm, and activate your purpose through small, consistent steps. Whether you're recovering from rejection, stuck at a crossroads, or ready to create something new, this journey is for you.

Each day includes a short reflection, a powerful prompt, and one simple action. You don't need perfection, just honesty, courage, and a little bit of faith.

Let's begin.

Day 1: You Are Not Behind

Reflection: Your journey is unfolding at its own pace. Stop comparing your timeline to someone else's.

Prompt: What have you achieved that you haven't celebrated?

Action: Write a list of ten wins from the last year, even small ones.

Day 2: The Silence Doesn't Define You

Reflection: Being overlooked doesn't mean you're unworthy. Sometimes, silence is making room for clarity.

Prompt: Where in your life do you need to give yourself grace?

Action: Write a letter to yourself from the voice of compassion.

Day 3: Rejection Is Redirection

Reflection: Every "no" that hurt you may have saved you from what wasn't aligned.

Prompt: What closed door led you to a better outcome?

Action: Make a timeline of your biggest rejections and what they taught you.

Day 4: Purpose Isn't Always Loud

Reflection: Purpose isn't just found in the spotlight. It's often in the quiet, consistent things you already do.

Prompt: What do others come to you for naturally?

Action: Ask three people what they believe your strengths are.

Day 5: Start Where You Are

Reflection: You don't need all the answers to begin. You just need a step.

Prompt: What is one thing you can do today to move forward?

Action: Do that one thing. Then write how it felt.

Day 6: Your Story Is Worth Telling

Reflection: Someone needs to hear what you've been through. Your story has power.

Prompt: What chapter of your life has shaped you most?

Action: Write a short reflection about that season.

Day 7: Identity Beyond Titles

Reflection: You are more than your job title or qualifications.

Prompt: Who are you when no one is watching?

Action: List five non-professional things you're proud of.

Day 8: Create, Don't Just Consume

Reflection: You weren't made to just observe. Your voice and ideas matter.

Prompt: What do you wish existed in the world?

Action: Start creating it—sketch, outline, brainstorm, or prototype.

Day 9: Trust the Process

Reflection: Growth doesn't always feel good, but it's necessary.

Prompt: Where are you growing right now, even if it's uncomfortable?

Action: Journal one area of personal or professional growth.

Day 10: Find the Lesson

Reflection: Every hardship holds a lesson—look for it.

Prompt: What past struggle taught you something valuable?

Action: Write a "thank you" to that experience.

Day 11: Look Around You

Reflection: The solution you're waiting for might already be in motion.

Prompt: What are you already doing that brings people together?

Action: List ways you're already having an impact, no matter how small.

Day 12: Let Go of the Timeline

Reflection: Purpose isn't always on schedule. Trust the delay.

Prompt: What are you pressuring yourself to achieve too quickly?

Action: Write a note of permission to take your time.

Day 13: Lead Without a Title

Reflection: Leadership is not about position, it's about influence.

Prompt: Where are you already leading in your community or home?

Action: Take initiative today in one area where your leadership is needed.

Day 14: Connect to Something Bigger

Reflection: We find strength in connection—faith, community, family.

Prompt: What values or beliefs keep you grounded?

Action: Spend ten minutes in reflection, meditation, or prayer.

Day 15: Courage Looks Like Showing Up

Reflection: Courage isn't about being fearless, it's about choosing to keep going.

Prompt: What's something hard you've done that required courage?

Action: Write a "bravery resume" of things you've survived.

Day 16: You're Allowed to Change Direction

Reflection: Changing your mind doesn't mean you've failed, it means you're growing.

Prompt: What dream or plan no longer fits?

Action: Release it—write a symbolic "goodbye" to that old vision.

Day 17: Keep Showing Up

Reflection: Consistency creates confidence.

Prompt: What would happen if you showed up daily for the next thirty days?

Action: Set a tiny daily goal and commit for the next week.

Day 18: Find Your Fuel

Reflection: Purpose is sustained by joy, not pressure.

Prompt: What energizes you, even when you're tired?

Action: Do something today just because it brings you joy.

Day 19: Don't Wait for Perfect

Reflection: Start with what you have. It will be enough.

Prompt: What dream are you waiting to be "ready" for?

Action: Do one imperfect action toward it today.

Day 20: Your Impact Is Already Happening

Reflection: You may not see the ripple effect, but it's real.

Prompt: Who has been positively influenced by you lately?

Action: Reach out and tell someone they matter.

Day 21: Say "Yes" to Yourself

Reflection: You've been waiting for permission. Give it to yourself.

Prompt: What dream or idea have you been sitting on?

Action: Write it down, speak it aloud, and take one brave step toward it.

You did it. This isn't the end, it's the beginning. The steps you take from here are yours to define. But you've proven one thing: purpose doesn't have to be found. It can be *built.*

#FromPhDToPurpose #21DayPurposeChallenge

www.ingramcontent.com/pod-product-compliance
Lightning Source LLC
Chambersburg PA
CBHW052149090426
42741CB00010B/2205
* 9 7 9 8 3 8 5 2 5 3 3 4 0 *